A Mind To Do Business

A Mind To Do Business

By
Phil Chambers
&
Elaine Colliar

ECPC Publications
(A division of Learning Technologies Ltd)

Learning Technologies Ltd

Published by:
ECPC Publications
A division of Learning Technologies Ltd
The Forge
New Invention
Bucknell
Shropshire SY7 0BS
United Kingdom

www.mindmaptraining.com
www.learning-tech.co.uk

First Published 2004

A catalogue record for this book is available from the British Library

ISBN 1-904906-00-1

Cover design by Yves Van Damme (Pangraphics Ltd).

Prepress and typesetting by Pangraphics Ltd, Cupar, Scotland.
Printed and bound by MMS Almac Ltd, Keith, Moray, Scotland.

Dedication

This book is dedicated to every business colleague who has ever thought that there must be an easier way to balance work, study and life. We hope we can show them that there is!

To my baby boy, James Daniel, the birth of whom has spurred me onto greater and braver things in my life than I would have ever dreamed possible.

Elaine Colliar

I also dedicate it to my late Mother, who was a constant source of support, and to my Father who has unstintingly offered invaluable advice and helped me to see my work from the layman's perspective.

Phil Chambers

Finally we would like to dedicate this book to the memory of our friend Ron Hain, BNI Regional Director, who died aged only 48 whilst this book was reaching its final stages. Ron taught us the true value of business realtionships, how to build a business through Word of Mouth Marketing.

ACKNOWLEDGEMENTS

Tony Buzan - For Originating Mind Mapping
Rod Dumbreck - For technical help
Anne Jones - For proof reading and support
Lady Mary Tovey - For encouragement and comments
Dominic O'Brien - Dyslexic genius & inspiration to all mnemonists
Dave Thomas - Memory advisor

Contents List

Contents Mind Map

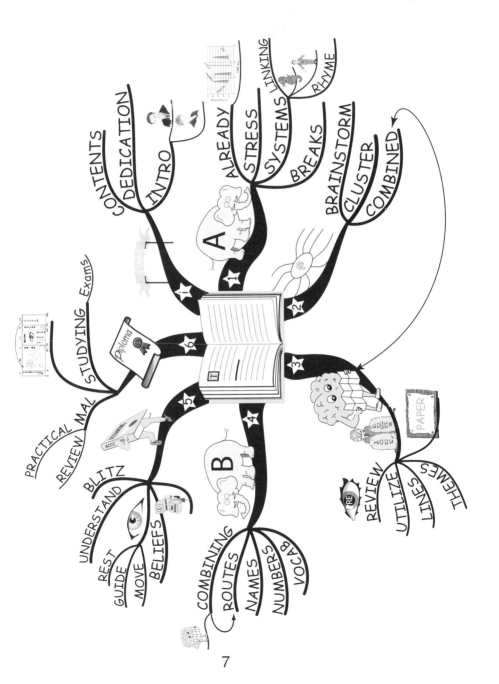

7

Elaine

Elaine Colliar is the five times World Mind Mapping Champion, reigning Mind Sports Olympiad Mind Mapping Champion and an International Grand Master of Mind Mapping. She hosts seminars in Mind Mapping, Memory, Mental and Financial Literacy around the world.

As a dyslexic, trained by the Buzan Centre several years ago, Elaine specialises in introducing these techniques, not only to multi-national companies but also to students at every stage of their career. Her passion is working with children with learning differences.

Starting her working life in the West End as a Stage Manager and Club Manager, she is now classed as a serial entrepreneur. Elaine has founded a string of companies including:

Btex Limited
Software and website development company, developers of the award winning www.streetmap.co.uk

Elaine Colliar Limited
A highly successful corporate training company
www.mindmaptraining.com

Building Success Ltd
A residential property investment company

Invest n Share Ltd
A company that teaches groups and individuals to utilise Mind Maps to maximise the returns they can achieve through investing in the stock market.
www.investnshare.com

She is an arbiter for the Mind Sports Olympiad, including the Memory and Speed Reading events. She was also co-author of the "Single Mom's guide to..." series.

Phil

Phil Chambers, a World Mind Mapping Champion, a five times Mind Sports Olympiad Medalist and International Master of Mind Mapping.

He has been a Buzan Licensed Instructor since 1995, trained by Tony Buzan (originator of Mind Mapping) and Vanda North (founder of Buzan Centres).

In addition to this, he is a certified Working Styles Analysis User, a Registered Accelerated Learning Trainer, a Practitioner of Neuro-Linguistic Programming (NLP), an Associate of the Chartered Institute of Personnel & Development (CIPD) and a member of the Professional Speakers Association.

Prior to entering the training profession, Phil worked as a computer programmer and has a BSc in Physics and Chemistry from the University of Durham. Drawing on this scientific background, he is one of the few people to successfully apply Mind Mapping to mathematics.

Phil is Chief Arbiter of the Memory Sports Council and scorer of the Mind Sports Olympiad Memory and Speed Reading events. He is a founder member of the Mind Sports Council and his contribution to Mind Sports won him the "Special Services to Memory" award in 1996.

His Mind Maps have been published in Hodder & Stoughton's GCSE and A-Level Revision Guides, "The Learning Revolution", "Teaching Pupils How To Learn" and "The Student Survival Guide".

You can contact Phil through his training company, Learning Technologies Ltd, at www.learning-tech.co.uk, which specialises in offering bespoke solutions enabling companies and individuals overcome problems and achieve their goals.

Chapter One
Memory Part A

Introduction

Imagine being the best client of a company. When you meet with them, they don't remember you are coming, they don't remember your name, they don't remember what company you are from nor what goods or services they supply to you. Would you continue to do business with such a company?

Imagine instead a meeting where you are greeted at the door personally, addressed by your correct name by someone who, not only remembers what you have been supplied in the past, but remembers enough about your company to recommend the best solution for you today. Would you continue doing business with this company?

More importantly – which kind of company are your clients going to choose to do business with? And what kind of company are you in?

The face of business is changing so rapidly that life-long learning has become essential. Our new portfolio careers bring the additional stress of having to continually update our skill-sets to keep our future employment prospects high. The necessity of juggling a full-time job and training requirements with family and home life can push some of us to breaking point.

What we need is the ability to learn something once, and to remember it accurately from that point forward. To create a powerful memory the first time we come across new information.

IN THIS SECTION WE WILL COVER THE FOLLOWING...

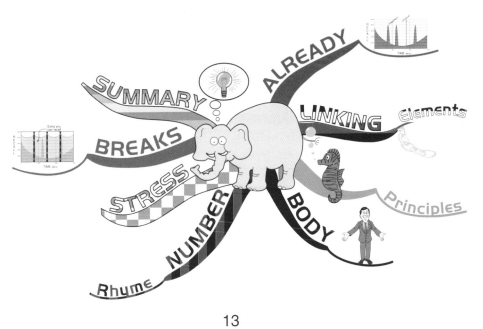

INTRODUCTION

WHAT YOU
ALREADY DO

LINK SYSTEM

SEAHORSE
PRINCIPLES

BODY SYSTEM

NUMBER
RHYME SYSTEM

BANISHING
STRESS

BREAKS

SUMMARY

What You Already do

Although the field of brain research is still relatively new, we already have a good idea of how effective memories are formed.

Over the years, we have tested thousands of people by challenging them to remember a list of 30 words that they hear only once.

Almost without fail, when we test their recall we find the same pattern emerging:

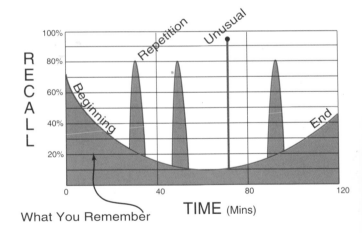

Our memories tend to follow a relatively predictable pattern – understanding that pattern and then applying it is the basis for building a great memory.

Think back – do you remember:

>   Your first kiss?
>   Your first day at work?
>   The 10th time you were kissed?
>   Your 40th drink?
>   The last person you kissed?
>   What time you left work yesterday?

You tend to remember 'first' things and the 'last' things much better than things in the middle of anything we do. The first time we come across information and the last time we do so are the most memorable. Beginnings and ends are memorable.

Unusual, outstanding or emotive events are also uniquely memorable. Think back and remember where you were, for instance when you experienced:

>   The news of the Twin Towers attack on September 11th?
>   The death of Princess Diana?
>   The night of the new millennium?

Things that we do frequently also create strong memories. Imagine replaying in your imagination the journey from your home to work. If it is a journey you have repeated frequently then you will have little trouble recreating many of the familiar landmarks in the correct order.

If you are very interested in something, it is much easier to learn and you remember more about the subject than if you are completely bored and uninterested. It is much easier for you to remember information about your favourite sporting hero if you are actually interested in the sport.

So, to immediately boost your memory, why not just do more of what the brain naturally does when it remembers?

>   **Create more beginnings and ends.**
>   **Include unusual and outstanding items.**
>   **Associate and repeat what you want to recall.**

The Link System

The Link System is a very simple but powerful technique. It takes each item in a list and links it to the next forming a chain of associations.

If the list contains abstract concepts. These need to be represented by pictures of objects.

As an example, let's try to memorise the "Ten Secrets of Abundant Wealth", from the book of the same name by Adam Jackson (published by Thorsons).

1. Subconscious Beliefs
2. Burning Desire
3. Definiteness of Purpose
4. Organised Action Plan
5. Specialised Knowledge
6. Persistence
7. Controlled Expenditure
8. Integrity
9. Faith
10. Charity

Picture the sea stretching out before you to the horizon. You spot a periscope breaking through the waves as a huge submarine surfaces: It's the bailiffs come to repossess a boat that hasn't been paid for. They're very hard working, in fact they're sub conscientious bailiffs (Subconscious Beliefs).

The boat owner doesn't want them to get their hands on his beloved boat and so burns hearts (Burning Desire) on the deck to deter them from boarding.

Leaping from the water beside the boat is a deaf porpoise (Definiteness of Purpose) balancing a clipboard on his nose (Organised Action Plan).

Attached to the clipboard is an old dusty book which, strangely, has a pair of intense blue eyes staring back at you – These are special eyes (Specialised Knowledge).

Crawling out from between the pages is a tartan clad spider, a descendant of the one who inspired Robert the Bruce (Persistence).

Scottish spiders are careful with their money. He has a padlock attached to his sporran (Controlled Expenditure).

A big wave knocks the spider off the book washing him ashore into gritty (Integrity) sand. A little girl called Faith scoops up the sand to make a sand temple (Faith) – more ornate than traditional sand castles.

Everyone who comes to look at it chooses to donate some money that goes into the (Charity) tin.

SEAHORSE
Principles

In simple terms, memories are pictures that you create in your head.

By using the following eight easy principles to add to these, you will be able to make unforgettable memories. The clearer and more detailed the picture – the easier it is to recall.

Senses

Making a memory more "multi-sensory" by using as many of your senses as you can (i.e. sight, sound, smell, taste and touch) will make the memory trace much stronger and easier to recall.

Exaggeration

By creating pictures that are larger, louder, smellier, sweeter, sourer and more tactile, you can boost what you remember.

Action

Create your images with as much action as possible. A full-colour horse, galloping through a field with its rippling muscles, flowing mane and high-pitched whinny is more memorable than a black and white image of a static horse.

18

Humour

Things that make you smile, giggle or groan – even bad jokes and puns will increase your enjoyment of learning and therefore increase your memory.

Order

Ordered items are easier to recall than those all jumbled up. One of the first ways we learn is when our carers tell us stories in which things must happen in a certain order.

Repetition

Repetition – especially at the appropriate times – boosts what you can remember. It reinforces the memory pathways in the brain, making it easier to remember what you are trying to learn. Every time you review, the memory becomes stronger.

Symbols

Using symbols boosts recall – especially as memories are pictures. Substituting abstract or ordinary items with extraordinary symbols will make them easier to remember.

Enjoy

Using your memory and your imagination to learn should be easy and fun. If you can make it fun to do, you will want to keep doing it – a well trained imagination will help make memorising a delight.

The hippocampus, a structure in the centre of the brain thought to be involved in memory is so called because of its SEAHORSE-like shape.

The Body System

Have you ever written down a list of things you need to remember – and then discovered that you can't remember where you put the list?

Here is an easy technique that helps you to remember anything that you would normally put on a list - ie shopping lists, to-do lists, etc.

The body has a number of parts in set locations that can act as places (or hooks) to 'hang' objects in your imagination:

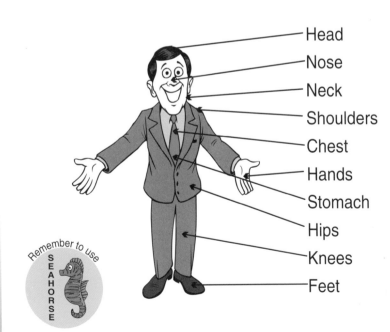

- Head
- Nose
- Neck
- Shoulders
- Chest
- Hands
- Stomach
- Hips
- Knees
- Feet

Remember to use
S
E
A
H
O
R
S
E

NOTE: This is a fabulous technique for remembering important points of a presentation.

For example, to remember the first three points in a presentation on money…

ON YOUR FEET:
A mortar board:
Explain trainer's background.

BETWEEN YOUR KNEES:
A giant five pound note talking:
Seminar title "Money Talks"

ON YOUR HIPS:
A Bull and a Bear:
Strategies for trading on the stock market.

The Number Rhyme System

Memories are pictures. You can remember a list, by linking each item to each number with a picture. Numbers are not naturally pictures so need to be converted into them first - one way to do this is with rhyme...

0
(hero)

5
(hive)

1
(bun)

6
(sticks)

2
(shoe)

7
(Heaven)

3
(tree)

8
(gate)

4
(door)

9
(wine)

Here are the first three items of a daily to-do list
linked to numbers and converted into pictures...

Talk to the HR Director about Graduate
training programme (Super-Hero dressed
as a graduate)

Complete monthly budget proposal
(Bun filled with money)

Call Mr Wood about office redecoration
(Shoe being painted by a man standing
on a plank of wood)

A couple of times each day, run through the numbers form 0 to 9 in
your head, recalling what is associated with each. If you have
completed a task, imagine the associated picture deflating like a
balloon leaving just the number's image with nothing associated to it.

You can reuse the list by 'overwriting' the information with new tasks
the following day.

Banishing Stress

Has your mind ever gone blank in the middle of an important presentation?

Have you ever had a client's name "on the tip of your tongue"?

You know that you know it but can't quite remember it and the harder you try to remember the more elusive the memory becomes. Then when you stop trying and relax the name just pops into your head.

What physically happens when you are stressed is that your brain goes into "fight or flight" mode - Faced with danger the best survival strategy inherited from our caveman ancestors was to fight or run away. Blood and oxygen are diverted from the upper part of your brain where memories are stored down to your muscles. So you're physically strengthened but mentally weakened.

The way to stop your mind from going blank is to avoid getting stressed. There are many simple relaxation techniques. Some people listen to music or practice Yoga, others study marshal arts like T'ai Chi. What you need to do to enter a state of relaxed alertness is this...

What we do

- Find somewhere quiet and comfortable to sit, away from distractions especially the phone.

- Close your eyes and breath in through your nose and out through your mouth. With each out breath giving a little sigh- 'ahh' - Counting slowly backwards from ten to one. With each number feeling the stress drain out of your body.

- Imagine being somewhere tranquil where you can feel relaxed and safe: A warm tropical beach, in a forest or in the mountains. Imagine the sights, smells, sounds, tastes and physical sensations as if you were really there.

- Spending as long as you like.

- When you're ready to return, count slowly back from one to ten, the scene fading with each number. When you reach ten, open your eyes and feel refreshed and relaxed.

The Power of Breaks

MYTH

In order for a meeting to be effective it must be strictly structured and no-one should leave until everything has been covered.

How many of your meetings last longer than an hour, more than 2 hours, more than 3 hours?

TRUTH

New business leaders have found that the most effective meetings are brisk, short and focussed. (After all, in meetings that last "forever" you actually work for a while, your attention drifts as you begin to daydream, then you tune in again – Not the most productive way to work). They work on the "little and often" principle.

You actually remember much more content if you break any activity down into little chunks than if you do it all in one go…

So you can recall more by working less. Don't work harder, work smarter!

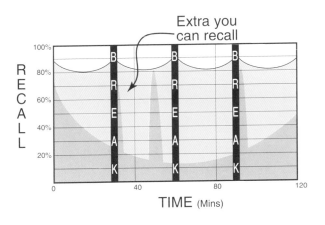

Extra you can recall

100%

R 80%
E
C 60%
A
L 40%
L
20%

0   40   80   120

TIME (Mins)

WHEN TO TAKE A BREAK

One of the most frequent questions asked during seminars is "We understand we should take breaks, we understand why we take breaks, but when should we take them?"

We all daydream – some of us even drift off at the most inappropriate points before fading back into the conversation and realising that we have missed something vital. This is entirely normal.

When you realise that your mind is wandering STOP and take a break.

Breaks don't necessarily need to mean leaving your desk and heading off for a cup of coffee, a change in task such as filing, responding to email or watering the office plant will suffice. A couple of minutes doing something else will leave you free to return a little refreshed and ready to take in some more information.

Summary

It is often said "good manners cost nothing" – and a good memory is one of the most courteous ways of respecting another person.

Not only remembering the client's name, but little personal details about them has enabled me to build several companies utilising the simple technique of "Word of Mouth Marketing".

Build strong relationships with clients by creating great memories of how interested you are in them and their businesses. How? By showing an interest; by always being the person asking 'How can I help you?'; by remembering the little things that mean a lot to other people. To be genuinely interested in them as people first and prospects second.

The benefit will be a thriving business. You succeed because clients constantly refer you to others in their field. Imagine, little or no marketing budget, little spent on advertising and a growing client base of loyal, and profitable, customers.

They remember you because you make a point of remembering them.

Chapter Two
Brainstorming

Introduction

With the ever increasing pace of change, no company can afford to rest on its laurels. You need to adapt and innovate just to stand still.

The companies that are succeeding now and will continue in the future are those that can constantly come up with creative solutions to problems and develop novel products and services.

Brainstorming is one of the most widely used, and most widely misunderstood, techniques for generating creative ideas. Used correctly, it can be a very powerful tool, but if not, it can be a drain on both time and resources with little, if any, reward.

We will show you the best way to Brainstorm for results. The technique quickly allows you to exhaust all the obvious ideas to reach the truly creative solutions that give your company a competitive advantage.

The winning companies will be those that mobilize the most brains.

Rikki Hunt
Chairman - Fuel Force

IN THIS SECTION WE WILL COVER THE FOLLOWING...

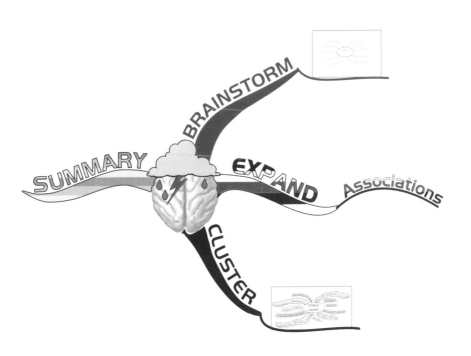

Brainstorming

Usually this means someone stands by a flipchart at the front of the room recording ideas shouted out as people come up with them.

This method has a number of disadvantages:

Despite the fact that it is understood that ideas should not be judged at the generation stage, the person recording the ideas will often summarise, misinterpret or even ignore some of the ideas from the group.

The process can be quite time consuming as every member of the group is focused on one idea at a time rather than each thinking independently.

As each member has to publicly express their ideas, individuals can be reluctant to participate for fear of being thought foolish. This allows the more forceful members of the group to dominate the session, restricting the number of ideas.

Because ideas are recorded as they occur, each idea is influenced by the previous one. This means that it is very easy to end up steering along a single narrow path, instead of producing many creative ideas, which is the whole point of the exercise.

A better approach is for each member of the group to draw a picture of the topic in the centre of a large sheet of paper with at least 10, or better still 20, lines radiating out form it. They then, very quickly, write their ideas on these lines, adding more if necessary before collecting the ideas together for further analysis by the group.

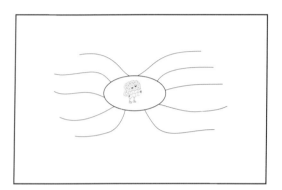

This has the following benefits:

♦ No ideas are lost through editing, as each member records their own ideas.

♦ The process is quicker as everyone is working simultaneously.

♦ There is no judgement of the individual's ideas, or fear of expressing outlandish suggestions.

♦ As each person starts their thinking from their own unique point of view, the ideas are immediately far more diverse.

♦ Having lots of lines encourages the generation of more ideas. The brain likes completion and so will come up with as many ideas as there are spaces on lines.

Expanding Associations

Be especially careful to remain open minded and receptive to ideas that might at first seem stupid or frivolous. Many brilliantly successful business ideas were the result of stupid initial thoughts…

STUPID IDEA	LED TO	BRILLIANT IDEA
Make boats with metal sails.		Racing yachts have aluminium wire woven into their sails 
Glue that doesn't stick		The 'post-it' note

A single idea can generate hundreds of ideas once the results of the group's individual brainstorms are collated. The starting idea is not in any way special or more fruitful than any other idea, so each new related idea could be the centre of a brainstorm in its own right.

You can draw new lines onto the end of the original brainstorm lines letting you include any additonal thoughts as they are triggered.

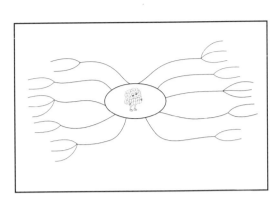

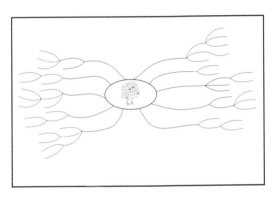

and so on...

Forever!

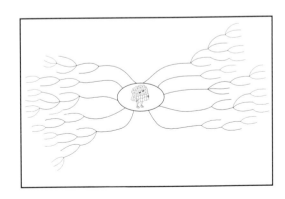

Clustering

Once you have taken your thinking wide with a brainstorm, it is often useful to improve the focus and clarity of your ideas by grouping them together under specific categories. You are not rejecting or editing ideas - Simply grouping them together into themes.

For example, if your brainstorm generated these ideas:

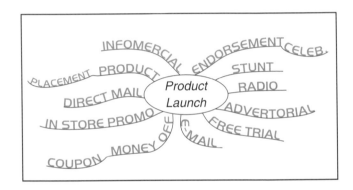

They could be grouped into the following themes:

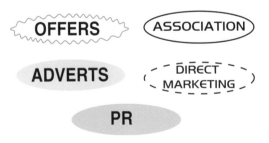

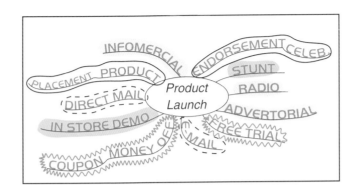

You may prefer to go through the brainstorming/clustering process before drawing a Mind Map allowing you to gather your ideas first, or you may prefer to launch straight into a Mind Map.

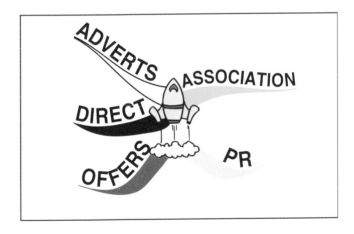

See the flow chart in the colour plates section showing this process in more detail.

Summary

Usually the announcement during training sessions that we are going to be looking at Brainstorming brings moans and groans from our delegates. Cries of 'Do we have to?', 'We already know how to do this' - or on one memorable occasion 'but it's so boring!' That of course is before trying this method.

Companies have realised for a long time that as we move forward into working in niche markets, new business ideas are to be found in the spaces between existing businesses. Our strength in the future will be creatively being able to identify these gaps.

In traditional brainstorming, we often become bored long before we come to the truly creative ideas. This new radiant way of brainstorming, working as it does with your natural way of thinking, keeps you engaged much longer – allowing you to explore far wider and find those unusual connections. (connections that happen after the ordinary ideas have been exhausted!)

Chapter Three
The Rules of Mind Mapping

Introduction

BENEFITS OF MIND MAPPING

As we get ever busier the sheer volume of information that passes over our desks every day means we need new business tools that can help us cope.

Mind Mapping is the most effective note making and note taking technique that we have found. It's adaptability to a multitude of applications means that this one technique, when mastered, enables you to cope in numerous situations, whether planning the launch of a new company, taking minutes, designing software, creating to-do lists or writing books.

Whether we regard ourselves as entrepreneurs, intrepreneurs or loyal employees, the ability to see the global perspective of a company is a huge business asset. Even more important is the ability to focus down on the detail within a company to make it more effective and profitable. Mind Mapping enables you to capture both sets of information within one document.

Mind Mapping is one of the world's most requested business tools within the corporate market. Skilled masters of this technique can command high salaries within organisations who seek the clarity, precision and detail that Mind Maps can offer.

Simply, Mind Maps work in harmony with the rhythms of the brain by using images, associations, space and colour to encourage thought processes to flow and to increase accurate recall.

They are powerful graphical representations of your thoughts and ideas – reflecting on paper the structure of your brain and how it processes information.

IN THIS CHAPTER WE WILL COVER THESE ASPECTS OF
MIND MAPPING:

THE RULES OF MIND MAPPING

CENTRAL IMAGE

It is important to create a unique and therefore memorable central image for each Mind Map that you create – especially if you are using the Mind Map for studying for professional exams.

If you feel that in the beginning the standard of your artwork lets you down, then get creative and copy, cut and paste, photocopy or print out an image from another source.

It is best to use as many colours within your central image as you can. We are programmed to remember better in colour than in monochrome, so three colours as a minimum gives your brain a better chance of recalling more accurately later on.

If you take the time to design a beautiful starting point for your Mind Map – you can immediately begin to create strong associations to the content and to recall the details more easily.

42

Fold with a margin

file by subject

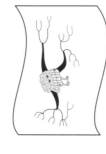

A3 paper

punch

PAPER

Use your paper in the landscape format - because our writing tends to be longer than higher, this leaves you more room for branching out with your associations.

Use blank paper - if you use lined or squared paper you may find you use the straight lines for writing on rather than flowing outwards in a radiant way.

Use as large a piece of paper as you can – A3 paper will leave you plenty of space to capture lots of detail on your Mind Map. For ease of filing and to be able to safely transport Mind Maps, why not fold and file them like we do?

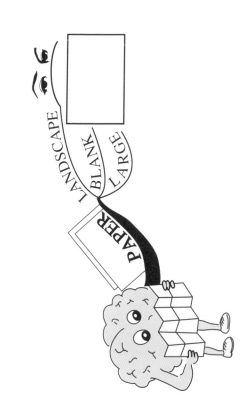

LANDSCAPE BLANK LARGE PAPER

WORDS

Mind Maps only use key words. They tend to be nouns and will usually comprise 5 – 10% of the words. This means that you will be capturing far fewer words making notes on a Mind Map than if you were taking "traditional" linear notes. Printing words (in upper or lower case) helps the brain to "photograph" the words more easily to recall at a later date. Using one word per line allows you to make more associations from each word and so improve your memory.

KEY WORDS

THEMES - IMAGES

Start by creating a unique image in the centre of your paper. After reviewing you will discover that you can recreate the Mind Map in your mind's eye. A unique image will help you to do this. Use at least three colours to make the image more attractive and hence memorable.

Don't draw a box around your central image. Leaving the image open with no boundaries drawn around it helps you to associate more freely and widely.

HIERARCHY

A Mind Map has a radiant hierarchy. The most important facts are clustered in close to the central image with the less important details out towards the edges. The order flows from the 2 o'clock position clockwise.

46

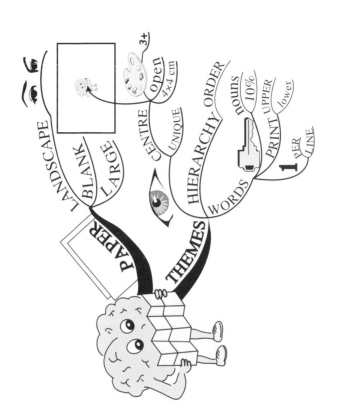

PAPER

LANDSCAPE

BLANK

LARGE

CENTRE

UNIQUE

open

4×4 cm

3+

THEMES

HIERARCHY ORDER

WORDS

nouns

10%

PRINT UPPER

lower

1 PER LINE

LINES

Make the length of each line equal to the length of the keyword or image on it. Too short and it won't fit, too long and you waste space! Make sure that each line connects to the end of the previous line and that the lines radiate out from the centre. Often if you leave a gap between lines you will fail to recall things 'downstream' of the break.

The lines should decrease in size and hence importance towards the outside of the Mind Map. At the centre they are thick like the branches of a tree, becoming thinner and thinner before tapering off into tiny twigs.

Try to use no more than 7 main branches on each Mind Map (short-term memory can hold 7±2 bits of information at a time) Less branches often lead to enhanced memory.

Using organic or wavy main branches in a Mind Map helps to draw the eye outwards. By using curved lines you are also best able to use the space on the paper, by curving the lines into the space available.

Using one colour for each branch provides an extra memory hook to increase the ease with which you can recall your information – "It's on the green branch"… "It's a long word, etc."

48

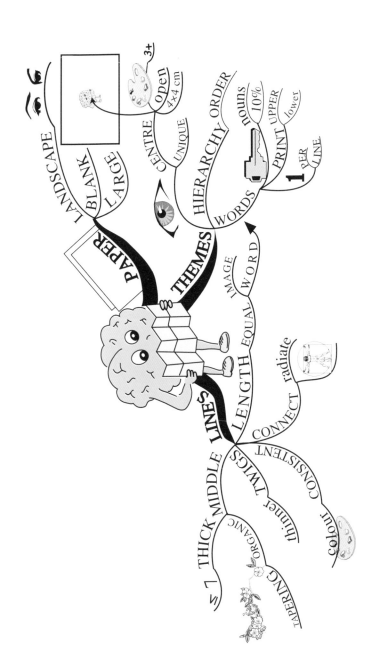

UTILIZE

Mind Mapping is a fun and creative way of making and taking notes. To keep the fun, keep your brain engaged and to help boost your recall, try to improve each Mind Map by increasing the use of each of these concepts every time.

If information is very important or relevant, you can use perspective to make the image look 3-dimensional rather than making it look flat – the information will then jump off the Mind Map and into your memory.

Make each new Mind Map just a little bit more beautiful to your own senses. Use lettering that you enjoy looking at, your favourite colours and images.

Have fun creating your Mind Map – if something is fun to do then you want to do more of it. So include humour, jokes, cartoons, puns (especially terrible ones)!

We are programmed to enjoy colour. All around us in the natural world there is vibrant colour. Rather than create boring, monotonous, monotone notes in black pen on white paper, rejoice in using multi-coloured pens, pencils, paints etc on the best quality paper you can find. Have fun experimenting with the hundreds of makes of pens on the market; fat pens; thin nibs; gel colours, glitter pens and scented pens. Use as many different types as you can to boost what you can remember.

ARROWS

One of the best ways to increase your understanding of say, a project and improve your accurate recall later is to become aware of how information is connected together.

The difference between someone who works IN a business and someone who adds value by working ON a business is their unique perspective -The ability to see the big picture and show how the different strands of the company connect together.

Arrows on a Mind Map enable you to see and understand immediately these connections.

You should not be surprised if the same word crops up on more than one branch of your Mind Map. This shows that the repeated word is a new theme running through the topic that you may not have seen had you been using linear notes. When you notice a word appearing on multiple branches you can reinforce the connection and hence your memory of the information by linking each occurrence with arrows.

Study the Art of Science and the Science of Art. Develop the senses and realise that everything is connected to everything else

Leonardo
da Vinci

As well as being used as a shorthand for particular concepts, codes can be used to indicate connections between related ideas. For example, if the same word occurs several times in a Mind Map you could either link each occurrence with an arrow or simply put the same code symbol (such as a star) next to each occurrence.

You can also colour code your Mind Map - For example, on a 'Task Schedule' Mind Map you can use highlighter pens to code urgent things in pink, things that rely on other people in blue and completed things in yellow. Similarly on a project plan Mind Map important or related concepts can be colour coded in the same way.

SENSES

Have you ever smelt a certain scent like the smell of fresh bread or a particular brand of perfume and been vividly reminded of a distant memory. It's not just smells that evoke powerful memories. Every experience is a combination of input from all your senses - So try to use words and images on your Mind Maps that evoke as many of your other senses as possible.

CODES

Letters and words are just codes that symbolise ideas - Likewise, road signs, icons on your computer, musical notes and numbers are also codes. Try to build up a library of your own code symbols that represent concepts that occur regularly on your Mind Maps.

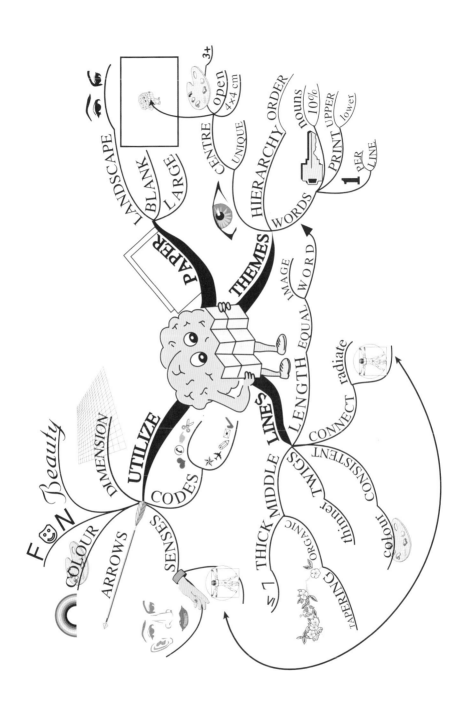

seconds. The entire review process consists of approximately 8 minutes spread over 3 months giving you almost perfect recall of all the information captured.

REVIEW

The strength of using Mind Maps is not only that they take so little time to create, but that they take so little time to review.

To help you keep track of when you need to review, date the Mind Map at the bottom and enter the review codes:

10, D, W, M, 3M

Which represent the time periods of 10 minutes, one day, one week, one month and finally 3 months. Simply strike through the appropriate code after you have completed each review.

A complex Mind Map containing all the data for an entire project can be reviewed in as little as 90

54

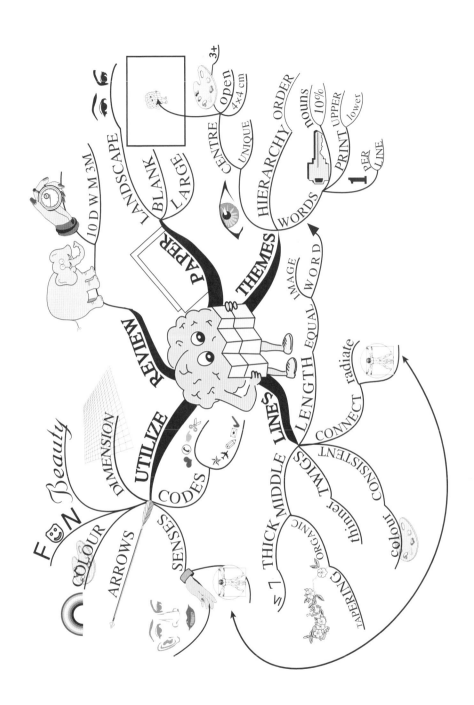

55

Summary

INTRODUCTION

THE RULES

SUMMARY

So you have seen the rules that you follow to create a Mind Map. These are all based on psychological research and many years of experience, so you should try to adhere to them whenever possible – especially if you are using Mind Maps to increase your understanding, boost your memory or study for professional exams.

Some of the time we may choose to do a rough Mind Map in a single colour e.g. a to-do list or a shopping list because we have no need to remember the information for a long time.

We have been caught in situations where we have had a fabulous idea but no blank paper and coloured pens with which to capture a 'proper' Mind Map. In that case what we usually do is create a Mind Map with whatever tools we can lay our hands on. Some of the best business ideas have been captured on napkins, beer-mats or on one memorable occasion the silver paper from inside of a packet of cigarettes.

These Mind Maps are still much more memorable than a list or set of bullet points – just because they reflect the structure of your thought processes. If they prove to be valuable we may actually redraw them in colour later.

Chapter Four
Memory Part B

Introduction

You should by now be comfortable using some of the simpler memory techniques such as the Body and Link Systems and using your ability to create strong memories by creating images using the SEAHORSE principles…

We will now show you some of the systems that the World's greatest Memory Champions use. These are not systems that are similar to the ones they use, but exactly the same – They just use them for recalling much larger chunks of information than you will need at the moment. To pass professional exams or remember clients' names and their details you need to be able to run for a bus – World Champions in the memory field need to be able to run marathons in record breaking times. Don't get disheartened if you feel you still have a huge way to go to get to where the champions are: By using the systems in this book you will still be better informed and able to remember information more efficiently than the majority of people around the planet.

If memories are pictures then the techniques in this section take you from an amateur photographer to a top movie director.

IN THIS SECTION WE WILL COVER THE FOLLOWING...

1   INTRODUCTION

2   THE ROUTE SYSTEM

3   MEMORISING NAMES AND FACES

4   LEARNING LANGUAGES

5   REMEMBERING NUMBERS

6   COMBINGING ROUTES AND MIND MAPS

7   SUMMARY

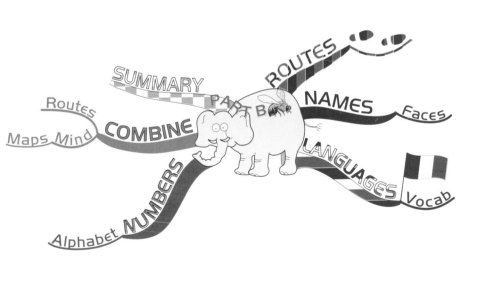

The Route System

This is one of the oldest recorded memory systems, used by the ancient Greeks and Romans, but as our brains have not significantly changed in what they are capable of in the last 2,500 years, what they did then is still as applicable today.

Routes work on the same basis as the Body System but allow you to remember far more informtation than the ten or so items that you are limited to on your body. You create an image of the information you wish to remember and link it, instead of to a location on your body, to a place along a very familiar journey or route.

Think of a route that you know well and can travel along in your imagination. For example, your journey to work in the morning or a trip to the shops. As you travel the route there will be a series of places or landmarks that you pass along the way. These will always be the same whenever you take that journey and will always be passed in the same order. These 'loci' as they are called, are used as hooks where you 'hang' the information to be remembered.

For example your landmarks could be:

| Front door | Gate | Traffic lights | Tree | Iron fence | Bench | Play area |

The process is as follows...

★   Prepare in your mind a well known route.

★   Select locations along your route in the order you come across them.

★   Using the SEAHORSE principles, create an image of the information you need to remember.

★   Attach the image to each location in order along your route.

★   Review your route thoroughly. You'll soon find that you are able to remember your information forwards and backwards, by travelling both ways along your route.

> Eight times World Memory Champion, Dominic O'Brien used this technique to set a new World Record by memorising the order of 54 packs of playing cards shuffled together.

Remember to use

S
E
A
H
O
R
S
E

Routes can be used with other systems such as the method for remembering numbers that we will look at later to make sure of order and sequence.

Names and faces

Remembering names and faces is one of the most common problems that people have. Once you have learnt a system to do this, you will immediately impress clients. Addressing someone by name creates the impression that you value them and their business. It helps to build a good relationship and encourages future custom.

The system, like so many others, is based on pictures. Look at the person's face carefully. Try to identify the most outstanding feature or features. Once you have done this imagine a caricature of the face with the particular features accentuated. Perhaps the person has large blue eyes, so you imagine them with huge bright blue shining eyes like the lights on a police car. Then take the name, form it into a picture and add this to the caricature of the face to make a single combined image in your mind. This means that the next time you see the face it will trigger the image and hence the name.

Some names have natural meanings that evoke pictures such as Hunter, Cook, Ball, Church, Wood, Park, Bell, Cooper (barrel maker), Smith (blacksmith), Collier (coal miner), etc. Others may need some more imagination to make their name into a picture such as Polawski (a polar bear skiing) or MacDougal (Dougal, the dog from the 'Magic Roundabout', wearing a raincoat).

You can also use famous people with the same name. For example: Jones (associate Tom Jones singing or, if you prefer, Catherine Zeta-Jones in one of her film roles), Parkinson (Imagine Michael Parkinson interviewing), etc.

So far we have only considered surnames. If you want to remember first names as well you can follow exactly the same process, just adding two pictures to the caricature of the face, one for the first name and one for the surname. Again, some names are easier than others. Lily, Rose, Poppy and Holly (plants), Robin and Martin (birds), Bill (an invoice), Jack (to lift up a car), Mike (a microphone), Bob (the weight on a plumb line, or a fishing float), etc. Your associations don't have to be exact – just close enough to trigger the right name: Julie (jewelry), Emily (an emery board), Bridget (a bridge), Lucy (loo seat!), Richard (money - riches), Brian (a briar).

Example:

Holly MacDonald

Exaggerate prominent features

Add images relating to the name to the image of the face.

We have provided some faces to practice the technique in the colour plates section of the book.

Learning Languages

Learning foreign language vocabulary is often a challenge for students struggling to associate the new word to something they already know.

To make this process easier, try linking each English word with its French equivalent by creating imaginary pictures or situations. If you apply the SEAHORSE principles and take care to use a situation or picture in which the link word closely matches the correct French pronunciation, you will find your recall is greatly enhanced.

The more fun you have creating memorable imaginary pictures, the easier they will be to recall, but you can also increase your recall by capturing your images in Mind Map form and following the suggested review process of 10 minutes, one day, one week, one month and three months. A large vocabulary in your long term memory will make it easier to locate the correct word when you are writing or speaking the new language.

We find that the biggest challenge when learning a european foreign language is to make sure that you learn the correct gender of the words. You can do this easily by creating strong images where you associate either a female or male character to the picture you are creating. When you recall the word you will also recall the person involved and so be able to recall the right gender.

This is especially important when you have to learn a language very quickly. You can learn gender and noun in one process rather than having to learn them in two separate parts.

In seminars we have been able to teach over 200 foreign words in one afternoon. What is more, students could still remember about 80% of the words when tested a month later. Here are some examples:

LE VIN -THE WINE

Big French boxer yanks open the door of a white van spilling thousands of bottles of wine onto the road. The bottles smash, drenching you in a pool of fruity red wine.

LE PAIN -THE BREAD

Freshly baked French bread being crammed into a big pan by a French boxer jumping up and down on the lid.

LA NAPPE -THE TABLECLOTH

A pretty French toddler dressed in a party frock. She is so tired that she puts her head down on a starched tablecloth to take a nap.

LA TASSE - THE CUP

The same pretty girl tying a tassle around a delicate china cup.

Numbers

Numbers are abstract concepts. They are hard to memorise because memories are pictures and abstract concepts are not.

To make memorising simpler, all you have to do is represent the number with a picture of an object. We saw in chapter one how to do this by rhyming. Rhymes work well for short numbers such as dates or to remember a numbered list but, if you have long numbers to remember, there is often too much repetition of the same pictures that can cause confusion.

Another way to convert numbers into pictures is to use the following code where each number is represented by a letter contained within a phonetic alphabet (This is called the Major System).

In order for you to learn the method, you must first learn a simple phonetic alphabet…. With a different consonant sound for each of the digits. I'll make this simple for you by giving you a 'memory aid' for remembering each one

Harry Lorayne
Memory Pioneer

66

Digit	Sound	Memory aid
0	s or z	first sound of the word "zero"
1	d or t	both have only one downstroke
2	n	written n has two downstrokes
3	m	written m has three downstrokes
4	r	fourth letter of the word "four"
5	l	Roman numeral for 50 is "L"
6	g	letter g turned around looks like 6
7	k	two 7's together look like a K
8	f	handwritten f looks like an 8
9	b or p	handwritten 9 turned around is like b or p

Each digit that you wish to remember will have a phonetic substitute. By stringing these sounds together with vowels you can create words, which become the images that you are able to recall easily.

To remember longer numbers you can join them together using a link system, as you did earlier with "Ten Secrets of Abundant Wealth" or use a route.

This is exactly the same system used by ex-firefighter David Thomas to set the Guiness Record for remembering the number Pi. After seeing another memory man on television demonstrating the system he decided to memorise Pi to 22,500 digits – just to prove it could be done.

Telephone Numbers

Telephone numbers are very well suited to this technique because they average about 11 digits and hence are too long to memorise effectively using the Number Rhyme System.

Here are some examples:

Learning Technologies Ltd - 07000 853276

We break the number down into groups of three digits:

070   008   532   76

We convert the number to sounds using the codes on the previous page:

070   008   532   76
SKS   SSF   LMN   KG

Converting these to words by adding vowels gives:

SeXy SouSaPHone LeMoN CaGe

(note 'X' has the same sound as 'KS', 'PH' has the same sound as 'F' and 'C' in cage has the same sound as 'K'. We ignore the 'N' in sousaphone because we are only concerned with the first 3 syllables)

The four words can be made into a picture which you then associate with the company by the setting - in this case a training room:

Elaine Colliar Ltd - 0781 6030586

Once again we break the number into threes:

078   160   305   86

We convert the numbes to sounds:

078   160   305   86
SKF   DGS   MSL   FG

Converting these to words by adding vowels gives:

SCruFfy DuCHeSs MiSsiLe FiSH

('C' in scruffy has a 'K' sound, likewise 'CH' and 'SH' are equivalent to a 'G')

Combining Routes and Mind Maps

ROUTES ON MIND MAPS

You create your Mind Map as usual, adding the various aspects of theory on the branches. You then add another branch on which you draw the first location along a route where you have recorded data related to the theory. Say, for example, you are studying employment law and you have memorised details of a relevant case on a route starting at your front door - Just draw your door on a branch:

When you come to review your Mind Map you will see the picture of the front door and run through the route In your imagination before moving on to the next branch.

MIND MAPS ON ROUTES

When Mind Mapping, you are encouraged to create a unique 'Central Image' to help you remember the Mind Map after your 5-times review. To mentally 'store' them you can associate the central image of each Mind Map to each place on a route. Recalling the location with the central image allows you to easily recreate the whole Mind Map in your imagination.

Your route could be as simple as a tour of your office. There are lots of locations around the room, these can be as small as the light switch or as large as the filing cabinet.

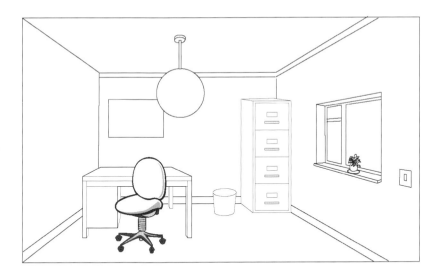

This gives you the ability to have information at your fingertips whenever you need it, especially useful if you are studying for professional exams.

Summary

We are both arbiters for the World Memory Sports Council – The world governing body for memory competitions. The most prestigious of these, the World Memory Championship, is worth visiting if you can. Details of dates and venues can be found on the official website (address at the back of this book).

You will be able to see, and meet, some of the best memorisers in the World, competing in a range of disciplines including memorisation of a binary number (just ones and zeros) over a thousand digits long, a three hundred digit number, spoken at one digit a second, memorised with a single hearing and many other impressive feats.

Until recently psychologists believed such things to be impossible and anyone claiming to able to memorise vast amounts of information was suspected of trickery. We now know that this is not only possible but, with enough practice, attainable by anyone. The National Institute of Health in America has spent three years and over a quarter of a million dollars investigating top memorisers' brains with the conclusion that they are no different to yours or mine!

Chapter Five
Speed Reading

Introduction

This is the chapter where we are going to introduce you to one of the most revolutionary ideas about processing information. Imagine if, instead of being stuck at a particular reading speed we could show you how to choose the appropriate speed for the information you are working on.

Even better, imagine if we could show you how to increase that speed by up to ten times, taking you from an average reading speed of 200 wpm to a comfortable 2000 wpm by using a series of simple steps with tools you already possess.

This technique will not only help you to read faster, but to read smarter, with improved understanding and recall. So speed is not won at the expense of comprehension.Evelyn Wood, American Speed Reading pioneer, explains...

> My reading technique is actually comprehension by accumulation. Speed is not most important but only through speed do you get good comprehension

IN THIS CHAPTER WE WILL COVER:

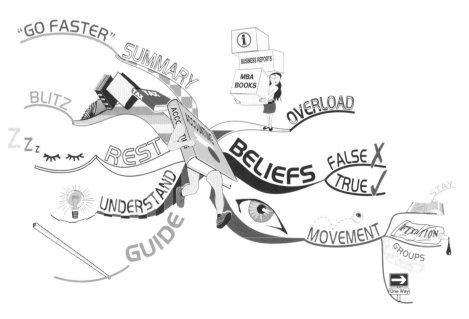

Information Overload

So how much written information is in your life just now?

Be honest. How much of it have you ACTUALLY read?

How do you know what's worth reading until you've read it?

Wouldn't it be great if you could read an entire book in an afternoon?

Or even better...

Get someone else to read the books for you and simply tell you the important parts?

Yeah right- like that's really goin' to happen!

Actually, it will

Do you know?

About 1,000 books are published internationally every day and the total of all printed knowledge doubles every five years.

Then there are reports, newspapers, magazines, journals, plus the massive explosion of material on the World Wide Web.

So how fast do I need to read to cope with this?

The average reading speed is between 150 words per minute and 240 words per minute.

The United Nations stated that to keep pace with all the information you would need to read at 400 wpm (but this was before the advent of e-mail, the Internet and texting)

An easy target to aim for is 1000 words per minute. However, with practice you can read at over 3000wpm

Beliefs

Have you ever been told

✗   Saying the words under your breath slows you down.

✓   **Saying words under your breath can help you remember - especially if you mentally shout out important bits.**

✗   Pointing at words with your finger is childish.

✓   **As we'll see later, finger pointing dramatically increases speed.**

✗   Read "slowly and carefully".

✓   **Reading quickly can increase your understanding.**

✗   Begin at the beginning and go through to the end.

✓   **You can learn more by just picking out important stuff from a book.**

✗   Go back and reread or look up anything you don't understand before you carry on.

✓   **Interrupting your flow reduces understanding and slows you down.**

✗   Read one word at a time.

✓   **You can easily read several words at a time.**

✗   You should understand everything you read.

✓   **100% comprehension is hardly ever necessary.**

✗   You can only read what your eyes are focusing on.

✓   **You can see an entire page with a single glance and take in more than you may think.**

✗   Never write on books.

✓   **A good way to engage with a book is to highlight words and make notes in the margins.**

Anne Jones has won the Mind Sports Olympiad Speed Reading tournament six times in a row.

What's more, she only uses the techniques that we'll show you!

The Eyes

A typical reader's eyes move something like this when they read a piece of text…

Jumping from word to word resting on each,

sometimes they skip backwards,

or even wonder off the page completely.

The way to speed up your reading is to avoid all these bad habits. Let us explain…

GROUPS OF WORDS

If you take in groups of words at a time instead of reading the words one by one you can greatly increase your speed. Even if you only took in two at a time that would double your speed and it's possible to take in six or more!

FIXATION TIME

A fixation is the name given to the stops in-between jumps when the eye recognises each word (or group of words). These last for anything between a quarter and one and a half seconds. If you can halve the time each fixation takes you can double your speed again!

ONLY GOING FORWARDS

Every time you back skip you waste time. So make an effort to only move forwards.

STAY ON THE PAGE

This sounds obvious but by keeping your attention on the page and not allowing your eyes and thoughts to wonder. You can improve your speed still further.

On the next page we'll give you a technique to help you to do all these things…

Guides

When you learned to read you probably used your finger to point to the words as you read them.

It was a good technique and worked very well until one day your teacher said something like, "Now you know how to read take your finger off the page because pointing at the words slows you down".

Surely a better thing to have done would have been to move your finger faster!

Your eyes are designed to follow moving objects. When you catch a ball, you don't see lots of static images - Your eyes follow and track it and help you move your hands into the right position (hopefully) to catch it.

Your eyes can move much more smoothly if they have something to follow. This could be your finger, a pencil or a chopstick. The benefit of a long slender guide is that it doesn't cover up what's coming next so you can see a preview of text up ahead before you actually read it.

The really great thing about using a guide is that it helps you apply the other techniques that we have just talked about:

GROUPS OF WORDS

By starting a little way in from the left and stopping a little way in from the right you are forcing your eyes to take in groups of words at the start and end of lines.

FIXATION TIME

The faster you move the guide the shorter your fixation times will be.

ONLY GOING FORWARDS

You don't have to be a genius for this one!

STAY ON THE PAGE

Keep your guide on the page and keep your eyes on your guide.

THINGS TO AVOID

Don't "tap out" words as you read them - move your guide in a smooth flowing motion under the words.

Don't use your guide like a ruler as this stops you seeing what's coming up. Instead use it as a pointer, so your eyes follow the tip.

Understanding

No matter how fast you read, if you don't understand any of it then there isn't any point in reading it!

One of the benefits of speeding up is that you can actually improve your understanding.

Every word or idea can be the starting point for the brain to make lots of associations. If you read too slowly then you are giving your brain plenty of time to make many associations, most of which will have nothing to do with the text. The faster you go the closer you are to understanding the author's intent and associations!

Another way to boost understanding is to reread the text. If you're reading at twice your usual speed, you can read the text twice in the same amount of time.

Try not to make rereading a habit. It not only defeats one the the reasons for speed reading - to free up more of your time - but also reduces your concentration. Eight times World Memory Champion Dominic O'Brien explains…

In my act I memorise words called out by the audience. In theory, the longer I take, the clearer the image and so the stronger the memory, but if there's too long a gap between words it throws my concentration. Because I know I'm only going to hear each word once, it forces me to focus my mind more…

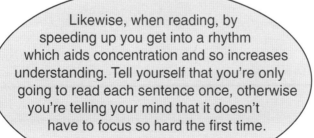

Likewise, when reading, by speeding up you get into a rhythm which aids concentration and so increases understanding. Tell yourself that you're only going to read each sentence once, otherwise you're telling your mind that it doesn't have to focus so hard the first time.

Resting The Eyes

Just like any other muscle the eyes need rest, especially when you have been reading or studying for a long while.

To refresh your eyes...

Rub your hands together briskly, until the palms are quite warm.

Lean forward on your elbows, cupping your hands over your closed eyes, resting lightly.

Think of blackness; black velvet; a black cat; deep dark night.

Rest like this for at least one minute.

Open your eyes and feel refreshed!

86

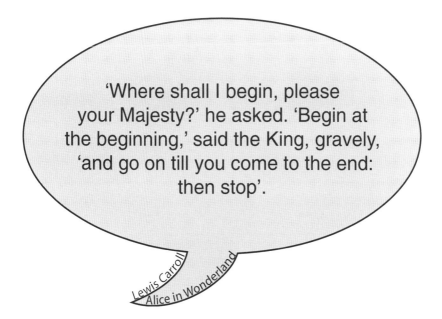

'Where shall I begin, please your Majesty?' he asked. 'Begin at the beginning,' said the King, gravely, 'and go on till you come to the end: then stop'.

Lewis Carroll
Alice in Wonderland

This advice may have been the best available in 1865 when Lewis Carroll wrote 'Alice in Wonderland'.

We now know that the best way to get the information from a book, especially a business book, isn't to read from beginning to end. Instead, work from the sections, to the chapters, to the headings in the text, to the details.

We'll show you how in the Book Blitz on the next page…

Book Blitz

With a group of colleagues
select a book each

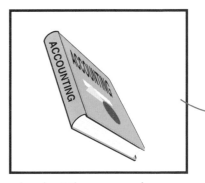

Look at the cover of your
book

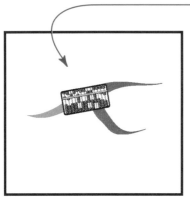

Sections become main
branches

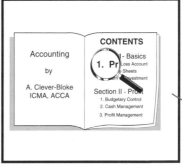

Find the chapters of the
book

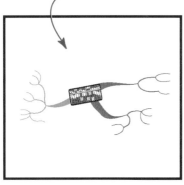

These become third level
branches

Speed Read the rest of the
text (if required)

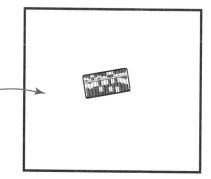

Decide on a central image

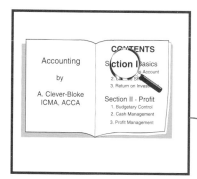

Find the sections of the book

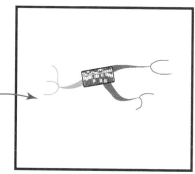

Chapters become second level branches

In each chapter find any headings in the text

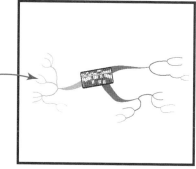

Add details

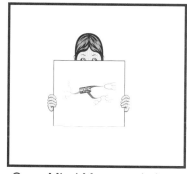

Copy Mind Maps and share with colleagues (each person explains theirs)

Celebrate

GO FASTER

The speed reading techniques can be summarised with the acronym GO FASTER...

Guide

Using a guide allows the eyes to move in a smoother way and helps with the other techniques.

Only Forwards

Back skipping wastes time and should be avoided. If you think you missed something keep going. It is very likely that you will understand what was meant by the context or the same point will often be repeated later.

Fixations Shorter

The less time your eyes spend resting on each word (or group of words) the faster you will read.

Allow Information to Come to You

Imagine reading as being like a sponge soaking up information rather than having to go out to grab it. This makes the process easier and much less stressful.

Stay on the Page

Keep your focus on the page. If you have problems concentrating make sure you take regular breaks and remember to rest your eyes when you start to get tired.

Take in Groups of Words

Practice increasing the number of words that you take in one go. If you can currently manage two, try three. You should eventually be able to get up to about six words at a time.

Enjoy

Everything, including reading is easier if it's fun. If you're not enjoying it, your thoughts will be elsewhere and you won't remember what you have read - So why did you waste the time reading it!

Reason for Reading

Before you start reading, decide what you want to get out of the text. Are there specific questions you need answering? Once you have a purpose, your brain will alert you to what you need - The information will "leap out" at you.

Summary

Time and again we find that people who are successful in business have one trait in common. They are more successful because they make better decisions based on greater knowledge and understanding. To become more informed they make reading a priority.

Most effective business people have large libraries of books they have carefully selected and digested over a period of time. They commit to continually expanding their minds and experiences by reading widely in their field.

The belief is that to become an expert you must read and understand one hundred books in your speciality. Now with the ability to read at the speed of your choice, or even to choose to divide your reading list with your colleagues, you can achieve this target easily.

In fact a structured programme of reading within an organisation is one of the hallmarks of a highly successful company.

Learning to speed read effortlessly and fluently has been claimed by millions of people around the world to be one of the most rewarding and significant events of their lives.

Tony Buzan
The Speed Reading Book

Chapter Six
Study Skills

Introduction

Learning as well as working is a challenge facing most people in business today. If you are in a field where you are expected to study for professional exams whilst continuing to work, what you need is a framework to make your studies as effective as possible.

As we learn more about how the brain works, we also learn more about how quickly the brain forgets. Using this knowledge, we can show you how to remember more by using a simple to apply review system.

This chapter deals with pulling together all the previous skills into an easy to follow, brain friendly form that can be applied to all of your studying, so that you can continue to work, to study and to have a social life.

IN THIS SECTION WE WILL COVER THE FOLLOWING...

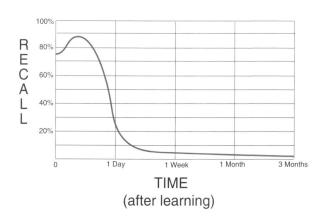
Memory after learning

People who consider themselves good at studying still 'forget' most of what they have learned within 24 hours. During that time they can lose 80-90% of the detail covered - Imagine, for every hour of study, they only remember 10 minutes worth of information.

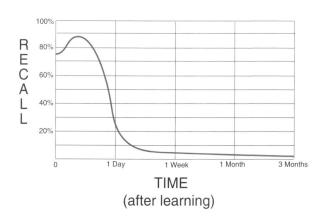

TIME
(after learning)

If you want to learn faster, work smarter and remember much more - here's how.

The easiest way to sustain your level of knowledge is to review it whilst your recall is at its peak. If you wait until your recall starts to decline then you have to relearn the information rather than merely review it.

96

Luckily, this doesn't mean reviewing everything you have learned every day. Five reviews is enough to transfer your knowledge into long term memory. The ideal times to review are after 10 minutes, one day, one week, one month and three months...

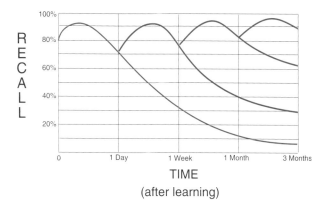

TIME
(after learning)

If you are using Mind Maps or one of the Memory Systems this entire review process can take less than 10 minutes in total. By starting to review as soon as you have learned something, you will never have to experience the panic of cramming at the last minute.

How to revise

1   Take your notes in a memorable way (we suggest you use Mind Maps)

2   Date notes and add review codes:
- 10 Minutes (10)
- Day (D)
- Week (W)
- Month (M)
- Three Months (3M)

3   Fold and punch Mind Maps for filing in your ring binder.

4   Name and number Mind Maps in sequence (eg Taxation 1, Taxation 2, etc)

5   File by subject

6   Write the Mind Map name and number into your diary for review tomorrow.

7   Repeat for :

- 1 week's time
- 1 month's time
- 3 months' time

8   On completion of each review strike through the appropriate review code on the bottom of each Mind Map.

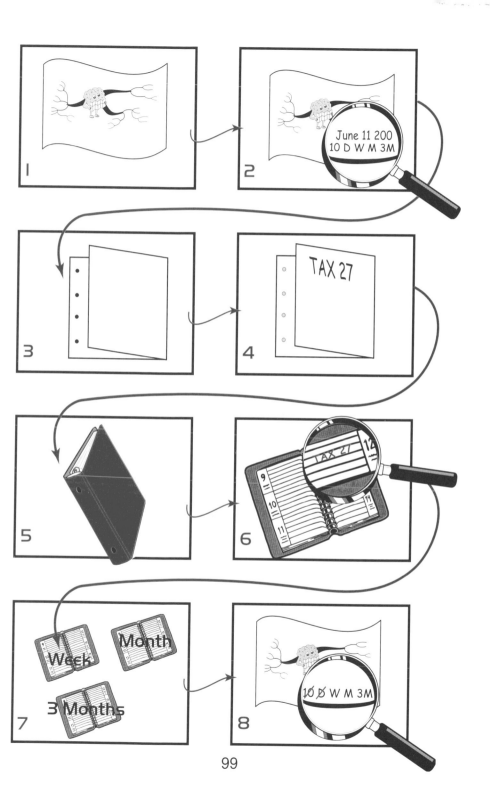

The Ideal Study Hour

We have developed the Ideal Study Hour over several years of working with people who need to get the most out of their study time. People who see the value of working within a highly effective and structured revision model.

It is based around all the principles of effective learning that we have covered so far in this book. You pay equal attention to reviewing information that you have previously learned, as you do to acquiring new knowledge. You do not have to re-learn material that you have forgotten because effective reviews transfer it into your long-term memory.

Material stored in this way is more accurately recalled in exam situations than less reliable last minute cramming. These memories are retained after exams and are available to you when required in the future.

Throughout the rest of this chapter you will learn how the Ideal Study Hour is constructed.

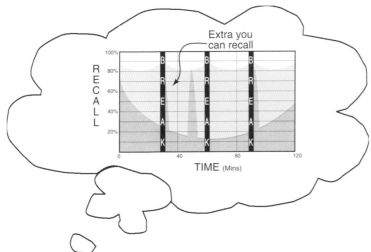

You can boost recall by taking breaks during your learning, so the Ideal Study System must include frequent breaks.

Do some gentle physical exercise in the first break to get better blood and oxygen flow to the brain

The brain is about 90% water by volume so grab a drink (ideally water) in the second break.

In the third break practice your relaxation technique to be better prepared for exams.

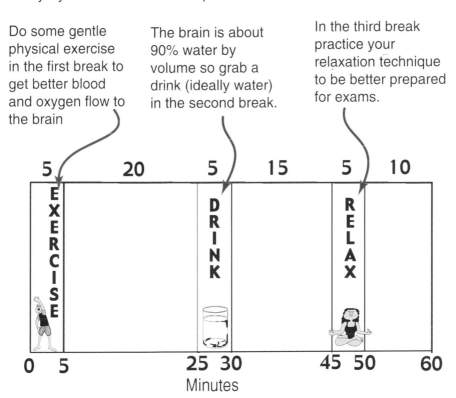

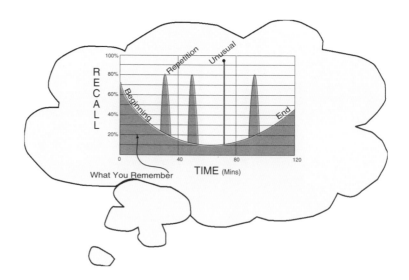

Spend the 20 minutes after your exercise using a study technique that works in harmony with your natural memory rhythms, ie lots of beginnings and ends, repeated and associated items and outstanding things.

Two examples of techniques that do this are Mind Mapping and the Route Memory System as both allow you to learn and recall large amounts of information easily..

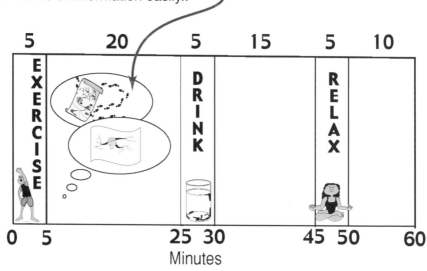

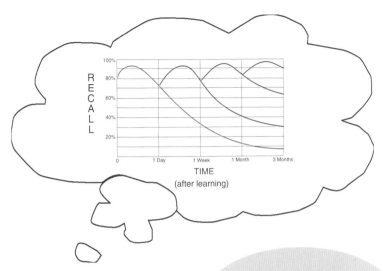

Spend the 15 minutes after your second break reviewing the Mind Maps or Routes from your files. Notes that you made yesterday, one week ago and one month ago, etc. This won't take long, for example you can review a Mind Map in a little as 90 seconds.

It's as important to review as to learn something new.

Linda Leckie
Student at LSE

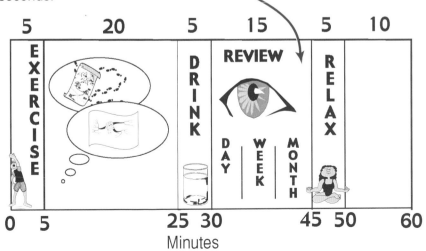

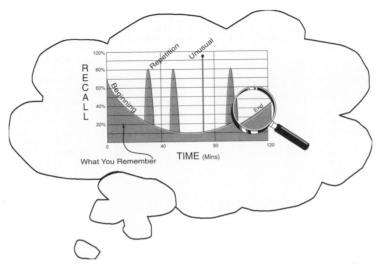

Because we recall more from the end of a session than from the middle, the last ten minutes is the ideal time for reviewing and completing the new work studied earlier. At this point you will see any gaps, additional connections or parts you do not yet understand.

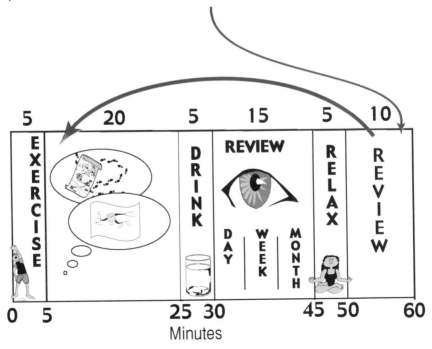

Summary

A couple of years ago we were approached by a group of three friends who were starting off down the route to prepare for taking their bar exams. They knew that according to the statistics from the past only one of them would be likely to pass, but that they were in for a few years of hard work and little pay for huge rewards if they were successful.

What they wanted to know was how to cope with the intense pressure of preparing for the exams whilst continuing to work and earning a living. They needed extraordinary study skills to be able to cope with the sheer volume of information they were expected to able to digest and understand.

Within a few weeks they had completely changed the way they were studying, they were now working much smarter instead of much harder and they were getting far better results.

It was a long road they travelled, but they did it. Actually, what we mean is that they ALL did it. They were all called to the bar and are now working on rising as fast up the ranks as their ambition permits. Even better, all three are involved in mentoring High School students to show them how they too can achieve amazing results.

What did they do?

Exactly what you have just learned.

Also by the authors...

The Student Survival Guide

Aimed at students of all ages, this book will show you the secrets of how to pass GCSEs, A-Levels and University courses with excellent grades but without spending more time studying. Imagine that, pass with straight A's and STILL have a social life!

Fourteen students from four South London schools approached us with a single burning ambition: "Show us what we need to get A's in our A-levels and we will do it" - and they did!

Despite three having dyslexia and one having cerebral palsy, ALL passed their exams with flying colours - An amazing 42 'A' grades between them. Even more fantastic, one young lady decided to study for A-level Spanish with only six months to go before the exams "Because learning was now so easy - I wanted a new challenge"

See how you too can achieve similar success.

Thank F**k it Wasn't Tammy Wynette - The Single Mom's Guide to Financial Freedom

The story of how Elaine went from being left at Heathrow Airport with her infant son and £70, to financial independence a mere three years later. This book will show you how she learned the skills necessary to achieve her dream. It will help you to set your own goals and learn how to achieve whatever you desire for your own life.

The Single Mom's Guide to... series of 'pocket' books:

- ... Designing your Life
- ... Financial Literacy
- ... Creating Assets
- ... Property Development
- ... Buy-to-let Properties
- ... Stock Market Investing
- ... Options Trading
- ... Building a Business

Training Services

The authors are available to run seminars in the following techniques...

Mind Mapping
Memory
Speed Reading
Creativity
Time Management
Accelerated Learning

For further information call:

Phil Chambers on **07000 853276**

phil@learning-tech.co.uk or visit **www.learning-tech.co.uk**

We also offer **Financial Literacy training** – Understanding how money works so that you can make your money work for you instead of always having to work for your money.

For further information call call:

Lawrie-Ann Blair on **01334 650 825**

info@InvestnShare.com or visit **www.InvestnShare.com**

Recommended Reading

MEMORY

Never Forget Names & Faces – Dominic O'Brien
ISBN 1903296811

Never Forget Facts & Figures – Dominic O'Brien
ISBN 1904292518

Never Forget A Speech – Dominic O'Brien
ISBN 190429250X

Never Forget Numbers & Dates – Dominic O'Brien
ISBN 190329682X

Learn to Remember - Dominic O'Brien
ISBN 0811827151

How to Pass Exams – Dominic O'Brien
ISBN 01904292399

Essential Lifeskills: Improving Your Memory - David Thomas
ISBN 0751348953

Use Your Memory - Tony Buzan
ISBN 0563537302

MIND MAPPING

The Mind Map Book - Tony Buzan
ISBN 0563487011

Use Your Head - Tony Buzan
ISBN 056337103

Get Ahead – Vanda North with Tony Buzan
ISBN 1874374007

SPEED READING

Remember Everything You Read: The Evelyn Wood Seven-Day Speed Reading and Learning Program - Stanley D. Frank
ISBN 0812917731

The Speed Reading Book - Tony Buzan
ISBN 0563383127

THINKING SKILLS IN BUSINESS

Creating a Thinking Organization – Rikki Hunt
ISBN 0566082306

RECOMMENDED WEB SITES

COURSES AND LEARNING TO LEARN

Additional Training
www.learning-tech.co.uk
www.mindmaptraining.com
www.mind-map.com

Speed Reading
www.speedyreader.co.uk

Accelerated Learning
www.learnfast.co.uk

FINANCIAL LITERACY

www.investnshare.com

MIND SPORTS

www.worldmemorychampionship.com
www.msoworld.com

Appendix
Colour Plates

COMBINING THE TECHNIQUES

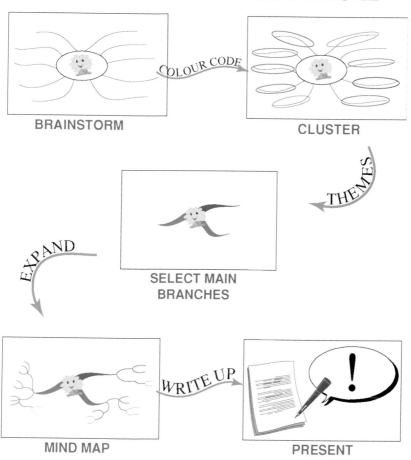

BRAINSTORM

COLOUR CODE

CLUSTER

THEMES

SELECT MAIN
BRANCHES

EXPAND

MIND MAP

WRITE UP

PRESENT

CELEBRATE

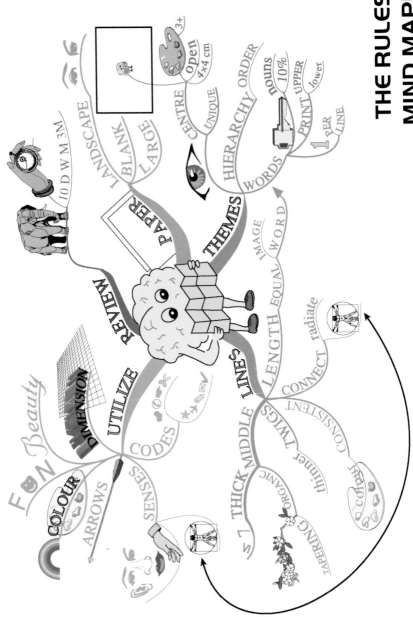

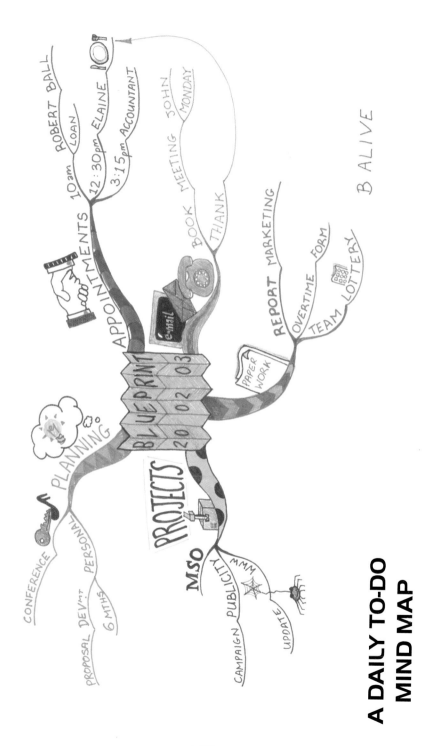

**A DAILY TO-DO
MIND MAP**

MIND MAPPED MINUTES OF A MEETING

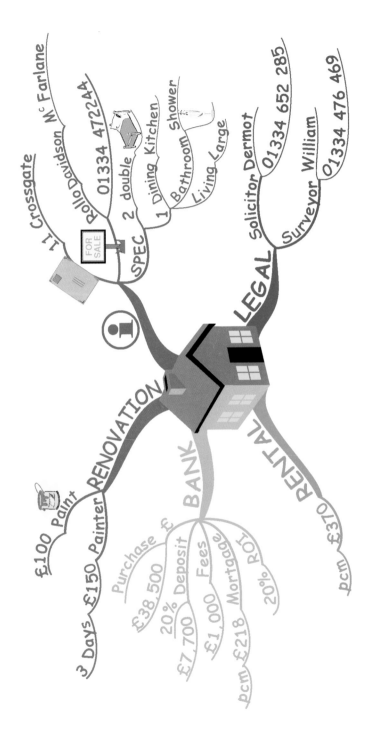

BUY TO LET PROPERTY ANALYISIS

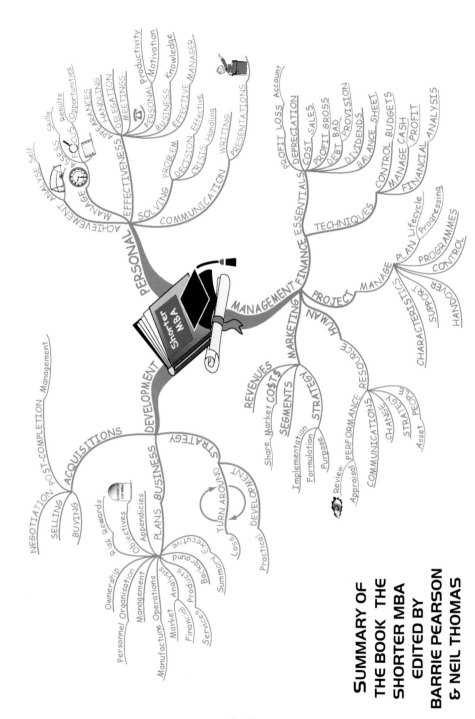

**SUMMARY OF
THE BOOK THE
SHORTER MBA
EDITED BY
BARRIE PEARSON
& NEIL THOMAS**

118

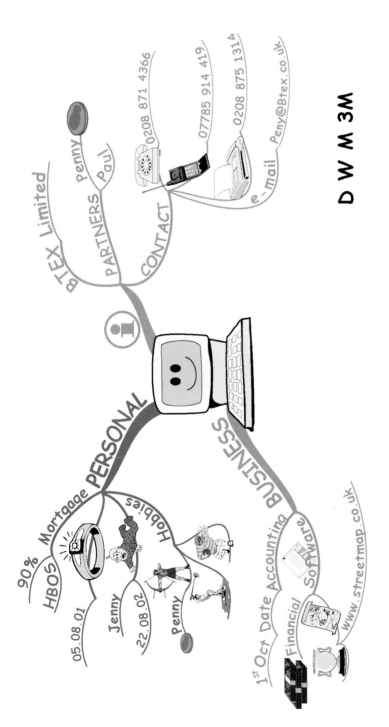

A CUSTOMER'S DETAILS MIND MAP

A MIND MAP FOR STOCK ANALYSIS

120

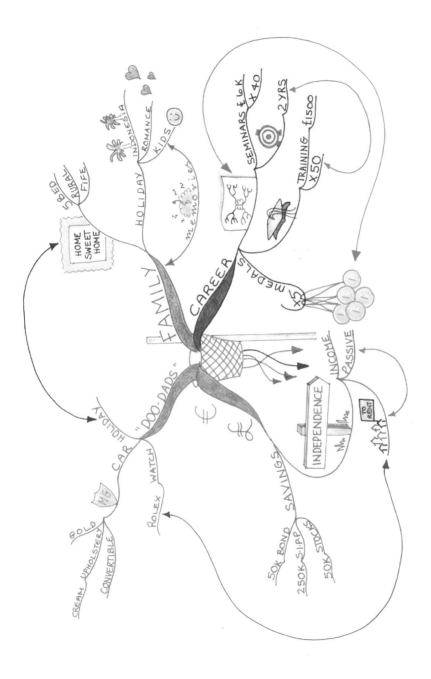

MIND MAPPED GOALS

**CREATIVE
MIND MAP**

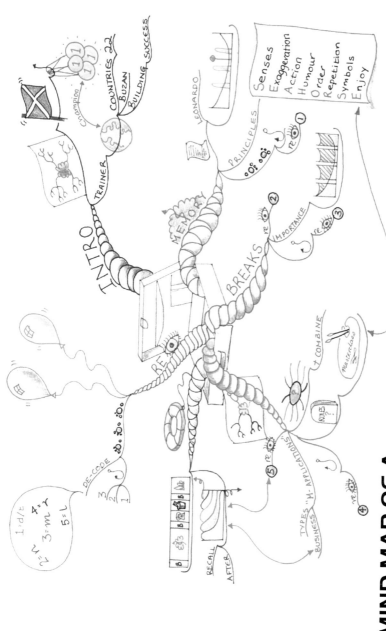

**MIND MAP OF A
ONE DAY SEMINAR**

123

STUDYING FOR PROFESSIONAL EXAMS

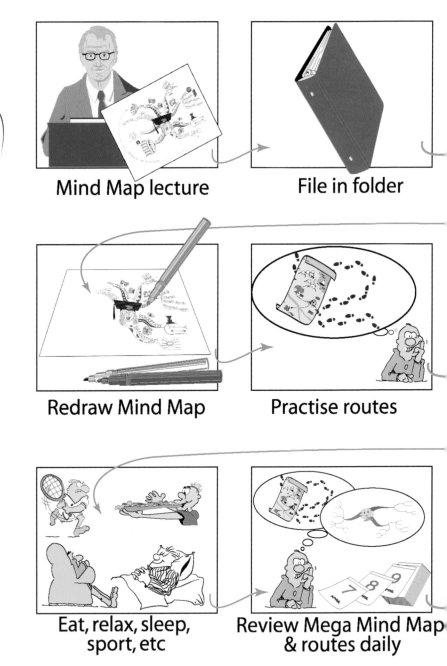

Mind Map lecture

File in folder

Redraw Mind Map

Practise routes

Eat, relax, sleep,
sport, etc

Review Mega Mind Map
& routes daily

Review: 10 minutes
day, week, month, 3 months

Route main points

Create Mega Mind Map

Review Mind Maps
and routes

Relax & good sleep
night before

Exam

Celebrate

THE IDEAL STUDY HOUR

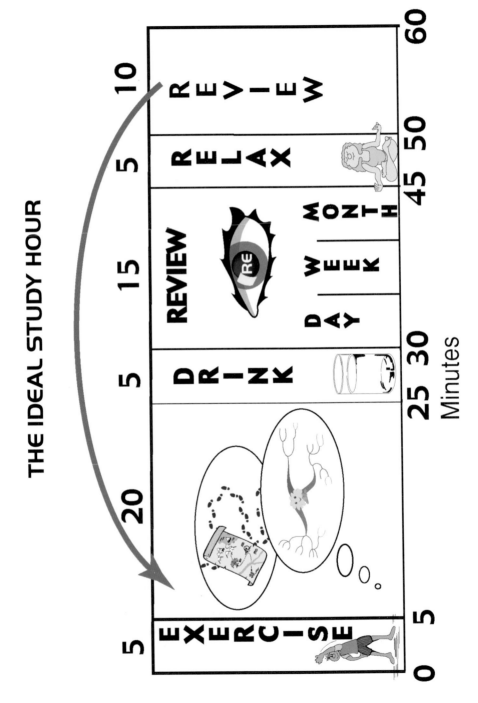

Minutes

NAMES AND FACES - MEMORISATION

Lillian Colliar

Lawrie-Ann Blair

Jim Colliar

Yves Van Damme

Graeme Skea

David Tyler

NAMES AND FACES - RECALL